(New Revised and Extended Edition)

CHORD DICTIONARY

By

Albert De Vito

T0058986

Contents
*NAMES OF CHORDS

Contents
CHORD SYMBOLS

KT 5-52R

*Chords are arranged alphabetically beginning with Ab.

Preface

In writing a CHORD DICTIONARY, one must consider where to begin and where to end. If including inversions and alterations of the Ninth, Eleventh and Thirteenth Chords, one could run into several unnecessary volumes. To eliminate this, Dr. Albert De Vito started off with a three note chord (Triad) and built from these the possible alterations of each chord which includes the Minor Seventh (flat seventh) interval from the Root and the Major Seventh, from the Root scalewise. On reaching the Ninth, Eleventh and Thirteenth Chords towards the end of the dictionary, one will find the same alterations may be made.

If a chord is combined with three notes, it may be played in three positions:— Root Position, First Inversion and Second Inversion. An example of this would be a "C" Chord (C–E–G) which is in the Root Position. The chord name, "C" is the Root. If "E" were the lower note of the chord, (E–G–C) it would be in the First Inversion. "E" is the Third of the chord. If "G" were the lower note of the chord, (G–C–E) it would be in the Second Inversion. In explaining this in classical terminology, in the key of C, this would be indicated by I, I_6, and I_4^6.

Chords are constructed in Thirds. (A knowledge of Major Scales will help for a better understanding. (page 49)The letter name of a chord is called the "Root" and the other notes are named by their distance in scale steps from the Root as a *third, fifth, seventh, ninth, eleventh* and a *thirteenth.* (pages 50 and 51)

1. A *Major Chord* is constructed by combining the root, third and fifth degrees of a Major Scale. (C D E F G A B C)

2. A *Minor Chord* is constructed by combining the root, a minor third and the fifth degrees of a Major Scale. (C D E♭ F G A B C)

3. An *Augmented Chord* is constructed by combining the root, third and the raised (augmented) fifth degrees of a Major Scale. (C D E F G♯ A B C)

4. A *Major* and a *Minor Chord* may be extended by a sixth, seventh, ninth, eleventh and a thirteenth. (The sixth is a thirteenth)

5. An *Augmented Chord* may be extended by a seventh, ninth, eleventh and a thirteenth.

6. A *Diminished Chord* may be extended by a seventh, ninth, eleventh and a thirteenth.

In extending the above chords, a note might possibly be doubled (duplicated) by an enharmonic tone. (same note but a different name) Also in using these extensions and alterations, some notes are left out. (See sections on the Ninth, Eleventh and Thirteenth Chords.

Enharmonic Chords are shown, B = C♭, C♯ = D♭ and F♯ = G♭. On the keyboard, the chords will have a sameness with a different spelling. The Enharmonic Chords (D♯ (E♭) and G♯ (A♭) are rarely used under D♯ and G♯ with the exception of D♯dim7 and G♯dim7.

Notice the chords in this dictionary are shown ALPHABETICALLY beginning with the A♭ chord and ending with the G chord.

A "+" or a "♯" (sharp) raises the pitch of a note one half–step. It is the very next key to the right, regardless of whether it may be a black or a white key. A "✗" raises the pitch of a note one whole step. It is called a *Double Sharp.*

A "–" or a "♭" (flat) lowers the pitch of a note one half–step. It is the very next key to the left, regardless of whether it may be a black or a white key. A "♭♭" lowers the pitch of a note one whole step. It is called a *Double Flat.*

We sincerely hope that this CHORD DICTIONARY, by Dr. Albert De Vito, will be a great aid in the adventure of music and that it will bring a better musical understanding to all that use it.

KT 5-52R

The Publisher

TRANSPOSITION CHART

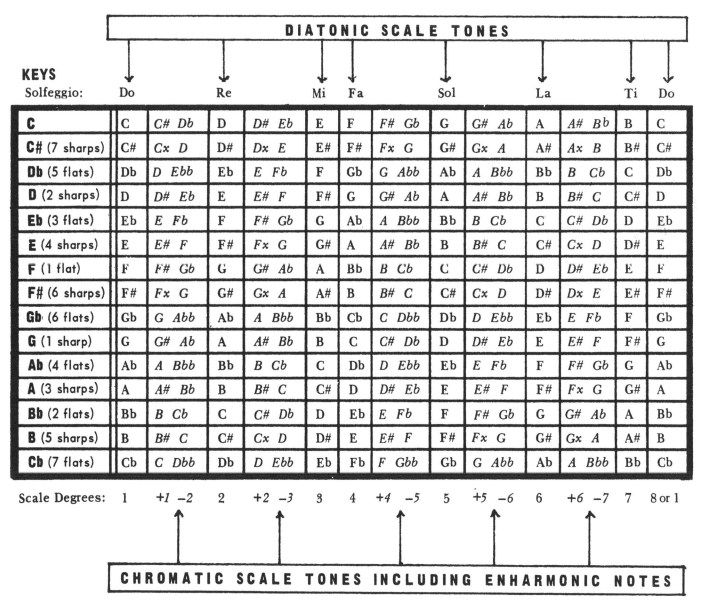

| **DIATONIC SCALE TONES** | | | | | | | | | | | | | |

KEYS
Solfeggio:

	Do		Re		Mi	Fa		Sol		La		Ti	Do
C	C	*C# Db*	D	*D# Eb*	E	F	*F# Gb*	G	*G# Ab*	A	*A# Bb*	B	C
C# (7 sharps)	C#	*Cx D*	D#	*Dx E*	E#	F#	*Fx G*	G#	*Gx A*	A#	*Ax B*	B#	C#
Db (5 flats)	Db	*D Ebb*	Eb	*E Fb*	F	Gb	*G Abb*	Ab	*A Bbb*	Bb	*B Cb*	C	Db
D (2 sharps)	D	*D# Eb*	E	*E# F*	F#	G	*G# Ab*	A	*A# Bb*	B	*B# C*	C#	D
Eb (3 flats)	Eb	*E Fb*	F	*F# Gb*	G	Ab	*A Bbb*	Bb	*B Cb*	C	*C# Db*	D	Eb
E (4 sharps)	E	*E# F*	F#	*Fx G*	G#	A	*A# Bb*	B	*B# C*	C#	*Cx D*	D#	E
F (1 flat)	F	*F# Gb*	G	*G# Ab*	A	Bb	*B Cb*	C	*C# Db*	D	*D# Eb*	E	F
F# (6 sharps)	F#	*Fx G*	G#	*Gx A*	A#	B	*B# C*	C#	*Cx D*	D#	*Dx E*	E#	F#
Gb (6 flats)	Gb	*G Abb*	Ab	*A Bbb*	Bb	Cb	*C Dbb*	Db	*D Ebb*	Eb	*E Fb*	F	Gb
G (1 sharp)	G	*G# Ab*	A	*A# Bb*	B	C	*C# Db*	D	*D# Eb*	E	*E# F*	F#	G
Ab (4 flats)	Ab	*A Bbb*	Bb	*B Cb*	C	Db	*D Ebb*	Eb	*E Fb*	F	*F# Gb*	G	Ab
A (3 sharps)	A	*A# Bb*	B	*B# C*	C#	D	*D# Eb*	E	*E# F*	F#	*Fx G*	G#	A
Bb (2 flats)	Bb	*B Cb*	C	*C# Db*	D	Eb	*E Fb*	F	*F# Gb*	G	*G# Ab*	A	Bb
B (5 sharps)	B	*B# C*	C#	*Cx D*	D#	E	*E# F*	F#	*Fx G*	G#	*Gx A*	A#	B
Cb (7 flats)	Cb	*C Dbb*	Db	*D Ebb*	Eb	Fb	*F Gbb*	Gb	*G Abb*	Ab	*A Bbb*	Bb	Cb

Scale Degrees: 1   +1 −2   2   +2 −3   3   4   +4 −5   5   +5 −6   6   +6 −7   7   8 or 1

| **CHROMATIC SCALE TONES INCLUDING ENHARMONIC NOTES** |

"x" is a Double Sharp. It raises the pitch of a note one Whole Tone.
"bb" is a Double Flat. It lowers the pitch of a note one Whole Tone.
"#" or a "+" raises the pitch of a note one−half step.
"b" or a "−" lowers the pitch of a note one−half step.

NOTE!
Each scale degree above may be treated in transposition as a CHORD as well as a Scale Note.
EXAMPLE: The note "C" in the Scale C could be considered as a C Chord, Cm, C dim, C6, C7
and when transposed to the Key of Eb, they would become:− Eb Chord, Ebm, Ebdim, Eb6 & Eb7.
If they were transposed to the Key of F, they would be:− F Chord, Fm, F dim, F6 and F7.

MAJOR CHORDS

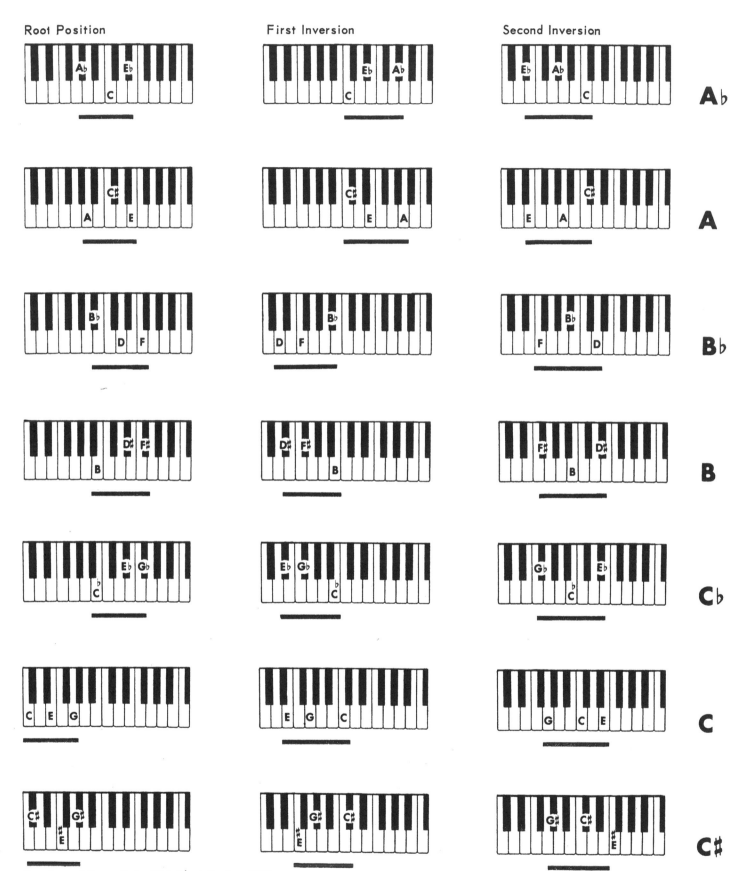

Consists of Root, Major Third and Perfect Fifth.

KT 5-52R

Root Position | First Inversion | Second Inversion

Db
D
Eb
E
F
F#
Gb
G

KT 5-52R

MAJOR CHORDS, SUS. 4

Root Position	First Inversion	Second Inversion	

Consists of Root, Perfect Fourth and Perfect Fifth.

KT 5-52R

Root Position	First Inversion	Second Inversion	
Db Gb Ab	Gb Ab Db	Ab Db Gb	**Db** Sus. 4
D G A	G A D	A D G	**D** Sus. 4
Eb Ab Bb	Ab Bb Eb	Bb Eb Ab	**Eb** Sus. 4
E A B	A B E	B E A	**E** Sus. 4
F Bb C	Bb C F	C F Bb	**F** Sus. 4
F# B C#	B C# F#	C# F# B	**F#** Sus. 4
Gb Cb Db	Cb Db Gb	Db Gb Cb	**Gb** Sus. 4
G C D	C D G	D G C	**G** Sus. 4

KT 5-52R

SEVENTH CHORDS

Root Position	First Inversion	Second Inversion	Third Inversion

Dominant Seventh Chord in the key of Db. In the keys of C# and C# minor, the spelling would be G#-B#-D#-F#.

  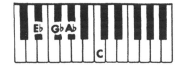  **Ab7**

Dominant Seventh Chord in the keys of D and D minor.

    **A7**

Dominant Seventh Chord in the keys of Eb and Eb minor. In the key of D# minor, the spelling would be A#-Cx-E#-G#.

  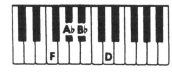 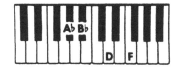 **Bb7**

Dominant Seventh Chord in the keys of E and E minor.

   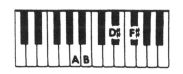 **B7**

Enharmonically as B7.

    **Cb7**

Dominant Seventh Chord in the keys of F and F minor.

    **C7**

Dominant Seventh Chord in the keys of F# and F# minor.

 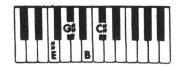 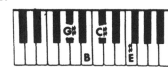  **C#7**

Consists of Root, Major Third, Perfect Fifth and Minor Seventh.

KT 5-52R

Root Position	First Inversion	Second Inversion	Third Inversion

Dominant Seventh Chord in the key of Gb.

  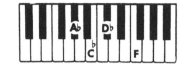  **Db7**

Dominant Seventh Chord in the keys of G and G minor.

    **D7**

Dominant Seventh Chord in the keys of Ab and Ab minor.

 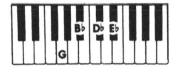 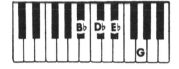  **Eb7**

Dominant Seventh Chord in the keys of A and A minor.

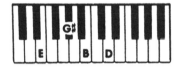    **E7**

Dominant Seventh Chord in the keys of Bb and Bb minor.

    **F7**

Dominant Seventh Chord in the keys of B and B minor.

    **F#7**

Dominant Seventh Chord in the key of Cb.

 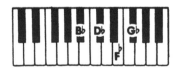 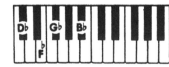 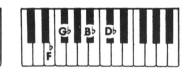 **Gb7**

Dominant Seventh Chord in the keys of C and C minor.

  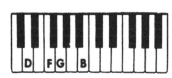  **G7**

SEVENTH CHORDS, SUS. 4

(The Suspended 4th may also apply to the 9th and the 13th Chords. The
Suspended 4th would be the 11th in the 11th Chord.)

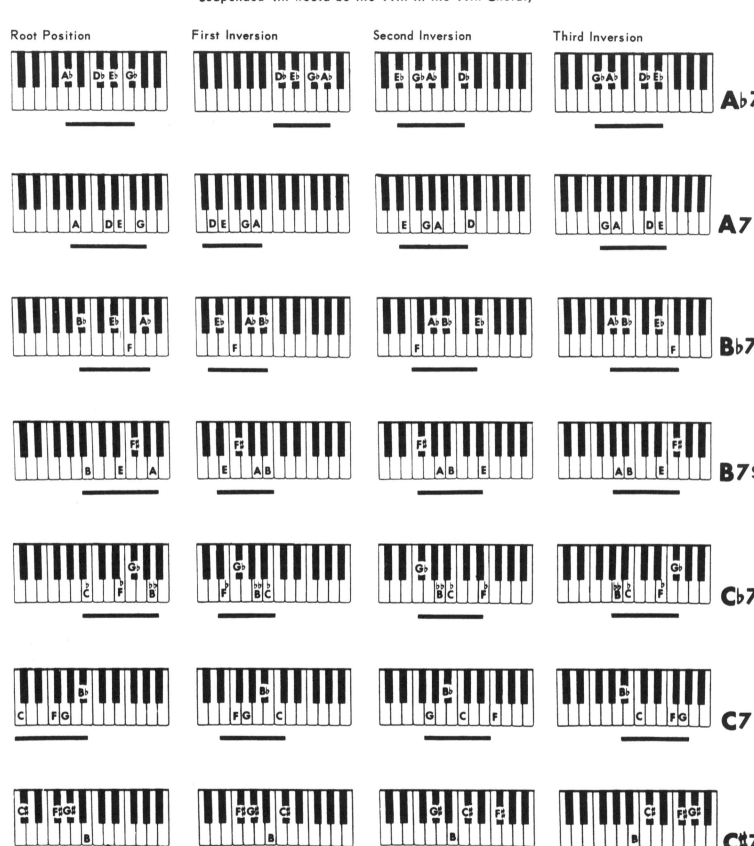

Consists of Root, Perfect Fourth, Perfect Fifth and Minor Seventh.

KT 5-52R

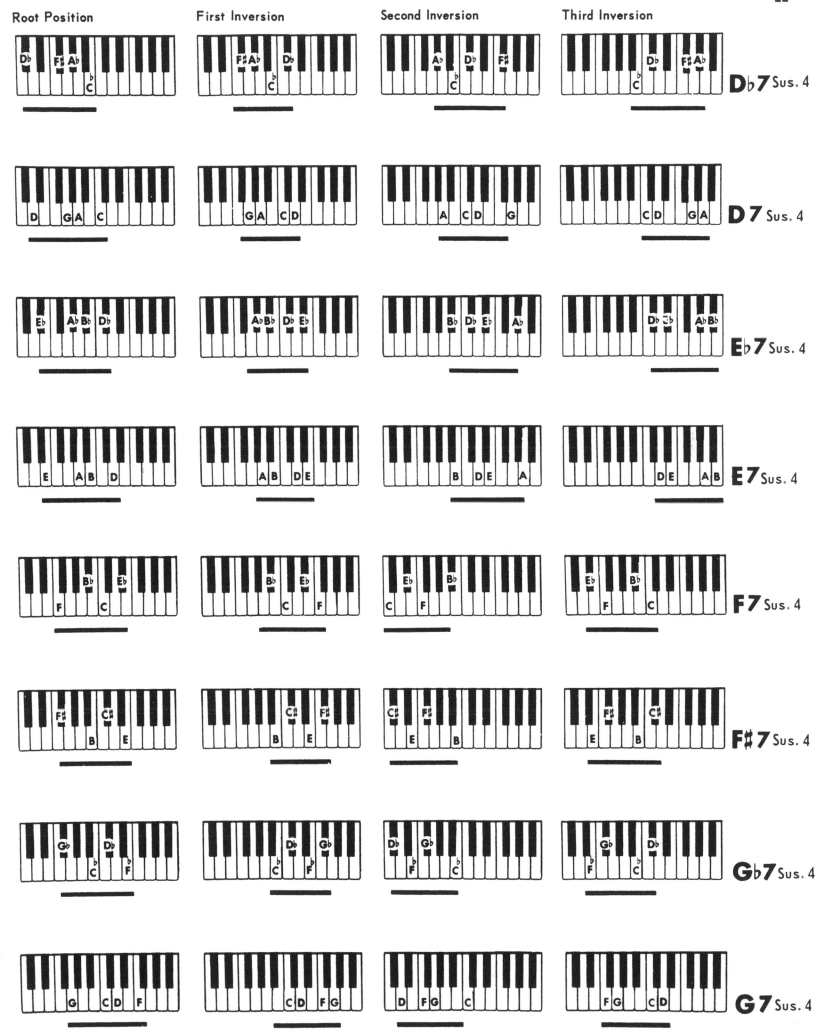

SEVENTH CHORDS WITH FLAT FIFTH

(C7-5, C7b5, C7-)

In reality, there are only six Seventh Chords with a lowered (diminished) fifth.

Ab7−5 = D7−5	B7−5 (Cb7−5) = F7−5
A7−5 = Eb7−5	C7−5 = F#7−5 (Gb7−5)
Bb7−5 = E7−5	C#7−5 (Db7−5) = G7−5

Root Position   First Inversion   Second Inversion   Third Inversion

Ab7b5

A7b5

Bb7b5

B7b5

Cb7b5

C7b5

C#7b5

Consists of Root, Major Third, Diminished Fifth and Minor Seventh.
The lower three notes of this chord, in the ROOT POSITION, can be a TRIAD WITH A LOWERED OR DIMINISHED FIFTH.
Ab−5, A−5, Bb−5, B−5, Cb−5, C−5, C#−5, Db−5, D−5, Eb−5, E−5, F−5, F#−5, Gb−5, G−5.

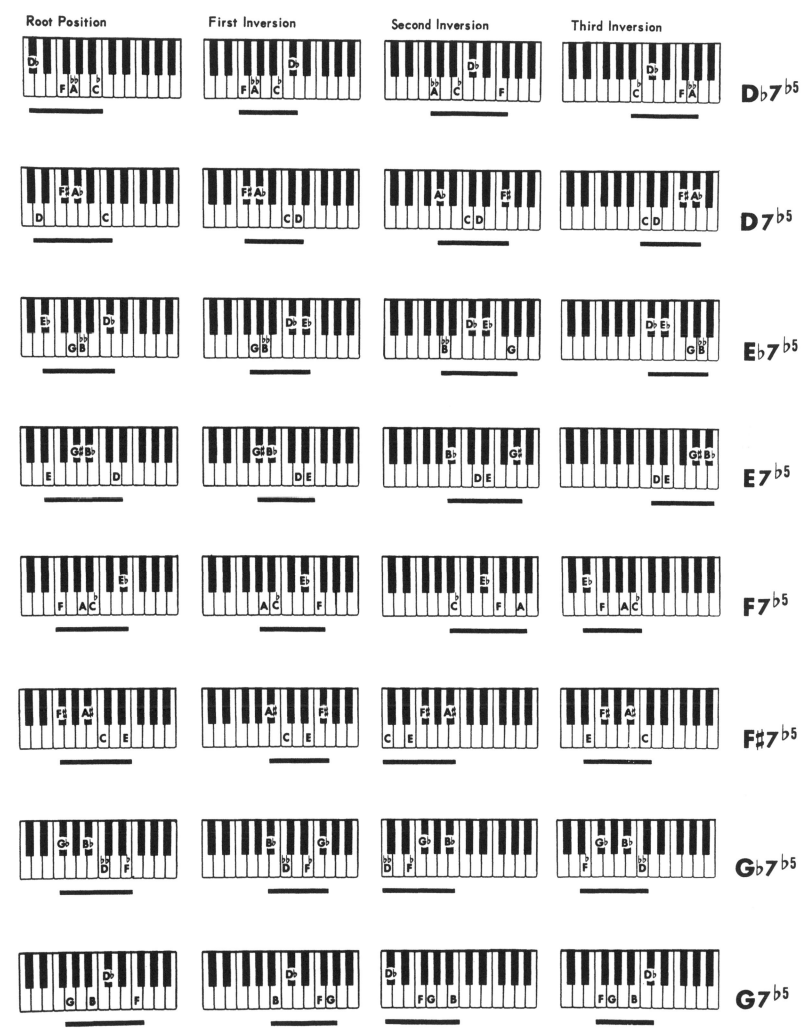

Root Position   First Inversion   Second Inversion   Third Inversion

Db7b5

D7b5

Eb7b5

E7b5

F7b5

F#7b5

Gb7b5

G7b5

KT 5-52R

MAJOR SIXTH CHORDS

The MAJOR SIXTH Chord sound the same as the MINOR SEVENTH Chord, p.18.

Root Position | First Inversion | Second Inversion | Third Inversion

Consists of Root, Major Third, Perfect Fifth and Major Sixth.

KT 5-52R

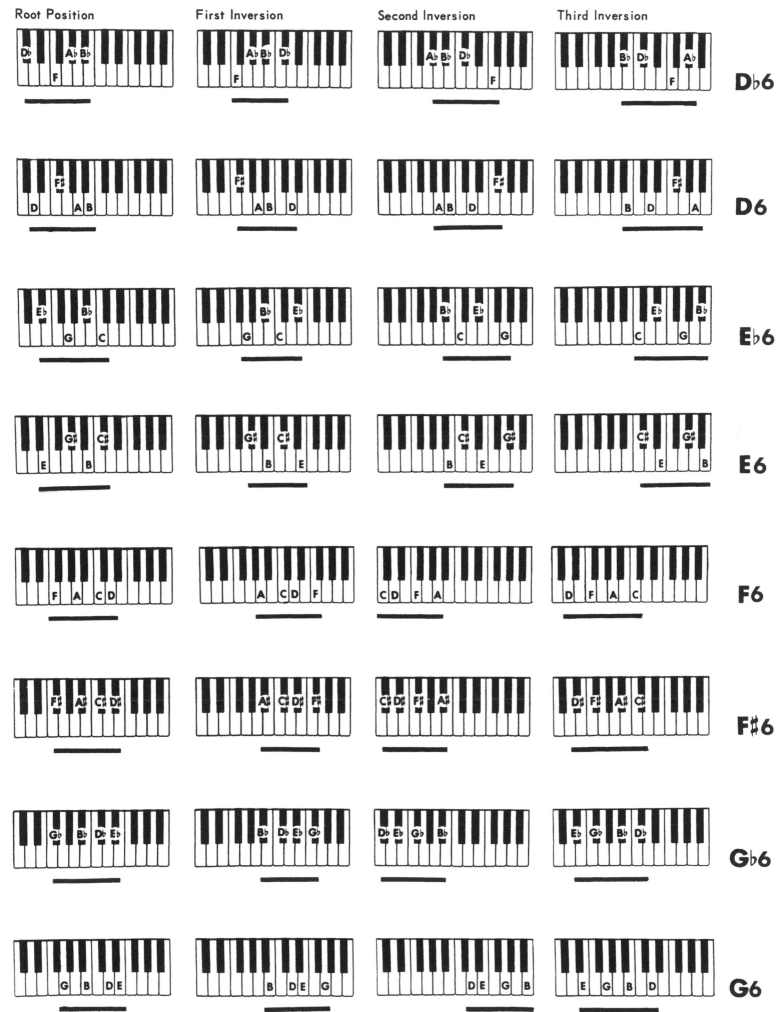

MINOR CHORDS
(Cm, Cmi, Cmin)

Root Position	First Inversion	Second Inversion	
			A♭m
			Am
			B♭m
			Bm
			C♭m
			Cm
			C♯m

Consists of Root, Minor Third and Perfect Fifth.

KT 5-52R

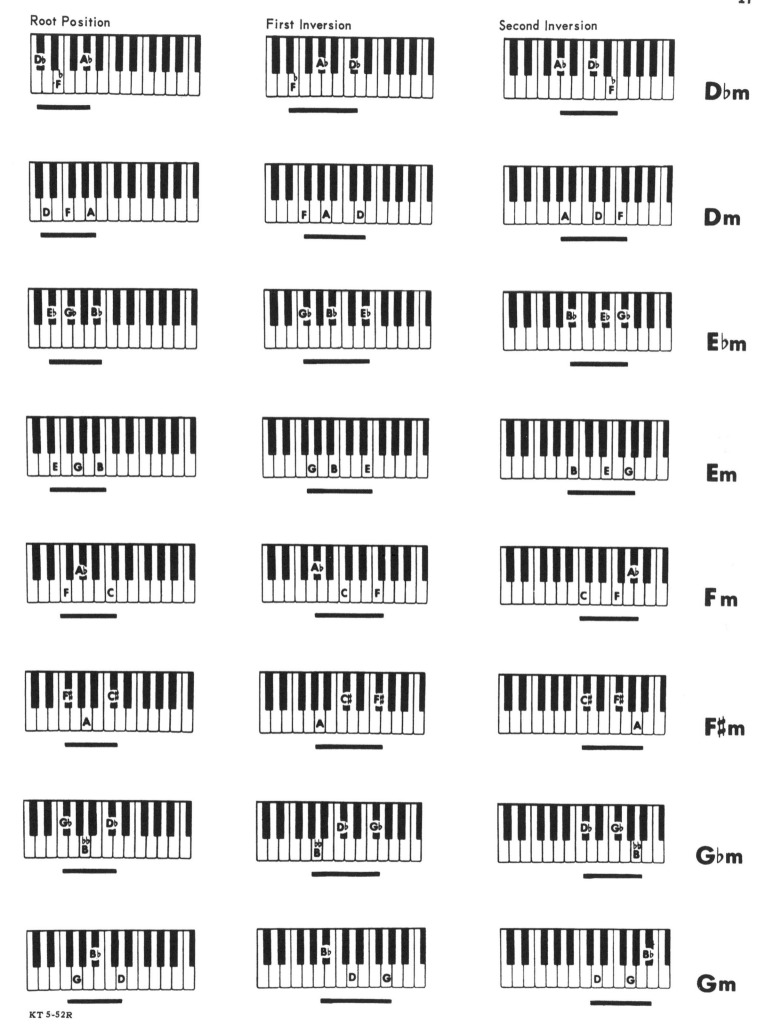

MINOR SEVENTH CHORDS

(Cm7, Cmi7, Cmin7)

The MINOR SEVENTH Chord sounds the same as the MAJOR SIXTH Chord, p. 14.

Root Position	First Inversion	Second Inversion	Third Inversion	
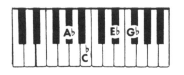	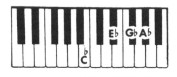	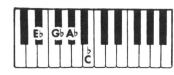	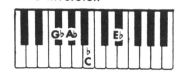	**A♭m7**
				**Am7**
	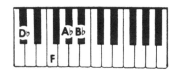	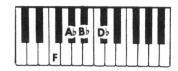	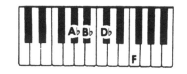	**B♭m7**
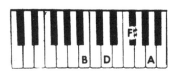			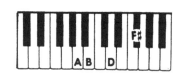	**Bm7**
	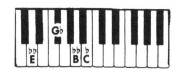	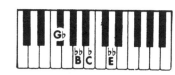		**C♭m7**
	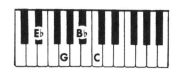	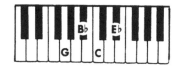	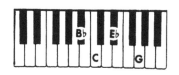	**Cm7**
	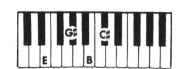	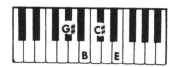	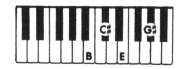	**C♯m7**

Consists of Root, Minor Third, Perfect Fifth and Minor Seventh.

KT 5-52R

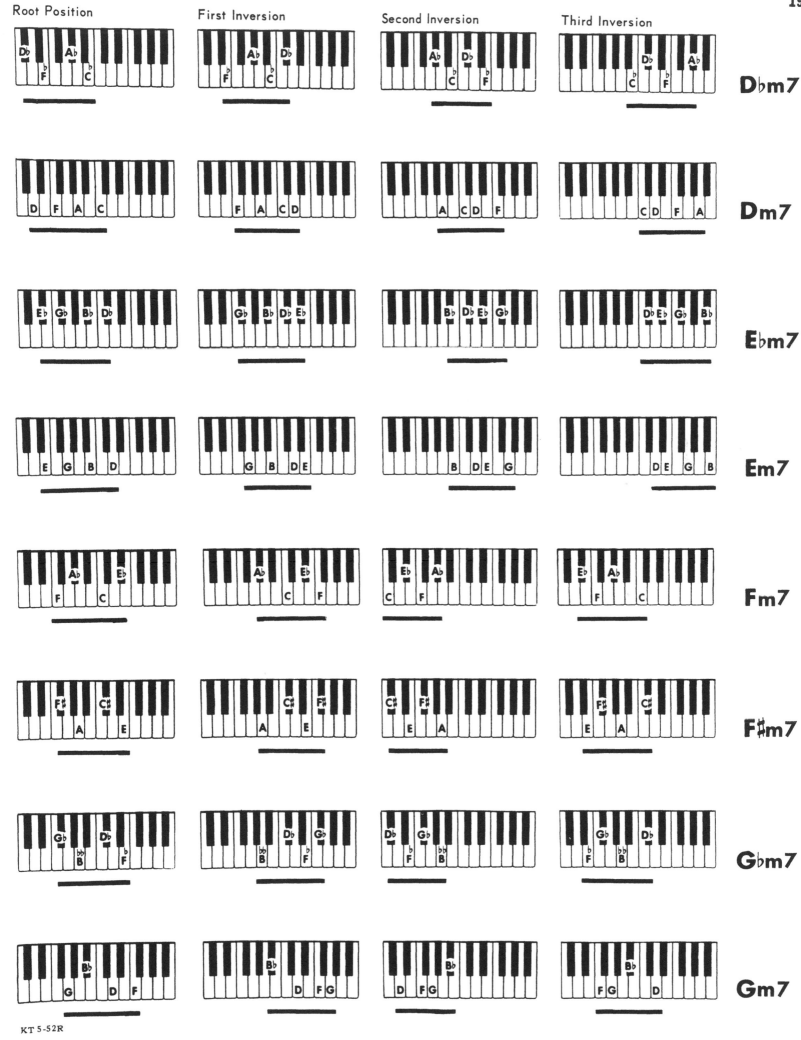

MINOR SEVENTH CHORDS WITH FLAT FIFTH

(Cm7-5, Cm7b5)

The MINOR SEVENTH Chord with a Flat (lowered or diminished) Fifth sound the same as a MINOR SIXTH Chord, p.22.

Root Position	First Inversion	Second Inversion	Third Inversion	
				Abm7b5
				Am7b5
				Bbm7b5
				Bm7b5
				Cbm7b5
				Cm7b5
				C#m7b5

Consists of Root, Minor Third, Diminished Fifth and Minor Seventh.

Sometime refered to as a "Half Diminished" Chord. Ø

KT 5-52R

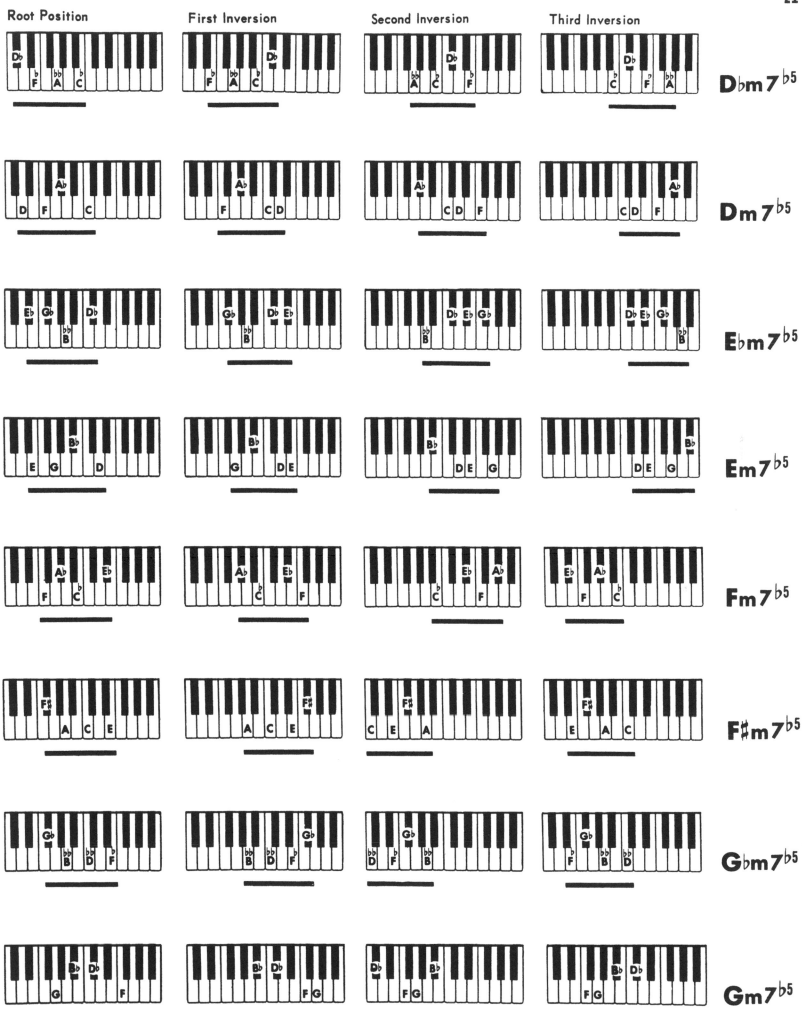

MINOR SIXTH CHORDS
(Cm6, Cmi6, Cmin6)

The MINOR SIXTH Chord sounds the same as the MINOR SEVENTH Chord with a Flat (lowered or diminished) Fifth, p.20.

Root Position	First Inversion	Second Inversion	Third Inversion	
				A♭m6
				Am6
				B♭m6
				Bm
				C♭m6
				Cm6
				C♯m6

Consists of Root, Minor Third, Perfect Fifth and Major Sixth.

KT 5-52R

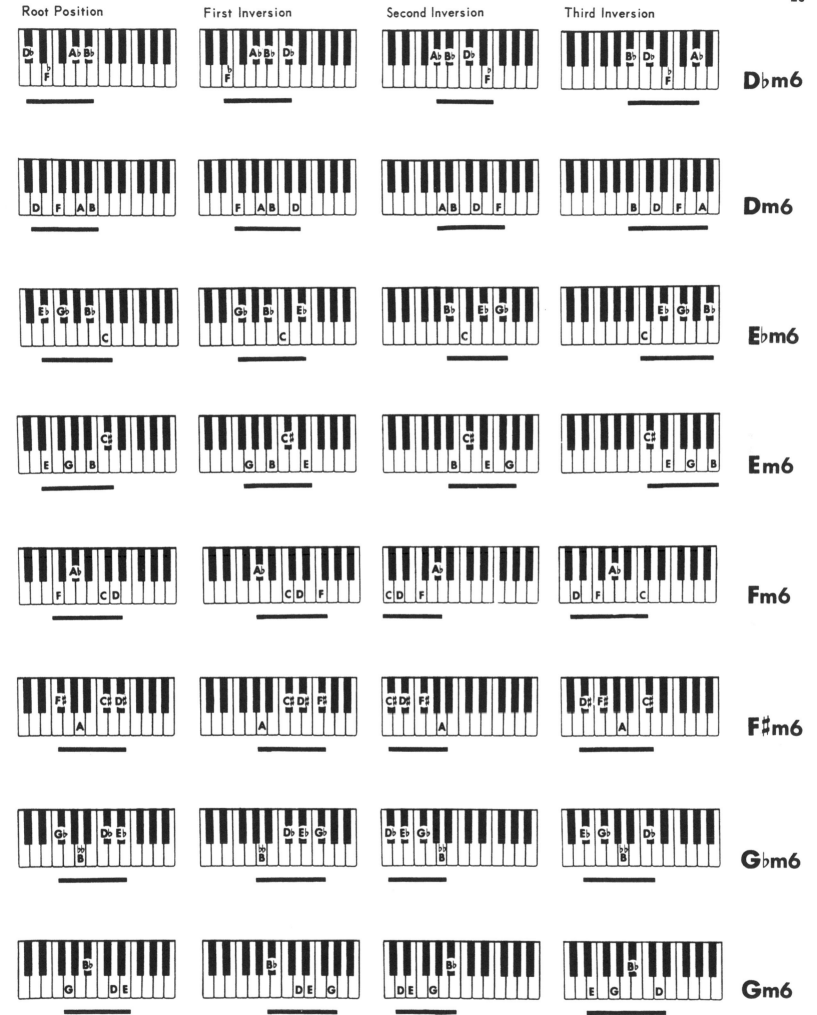

AUGMENTED CHORDS

(Caug, C+, C+5, Caug5)

In reality, there are only four groups of Augmented Chords.
1. Ab+, C+ and E+   3. Bb+, D+, F#+ and Gb+
2. A+, C#+, Db+ and F+   4. B+, Cb+, Eb+ and G+

Root Position | First Inversion | Second Inversion

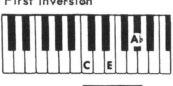 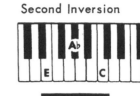

Ab aug

A aug

Bb aug

B aug

Cb aug

Caug

C# aug

Consists of Root, Major Third and Augmented Fifth.

KT 5-52R

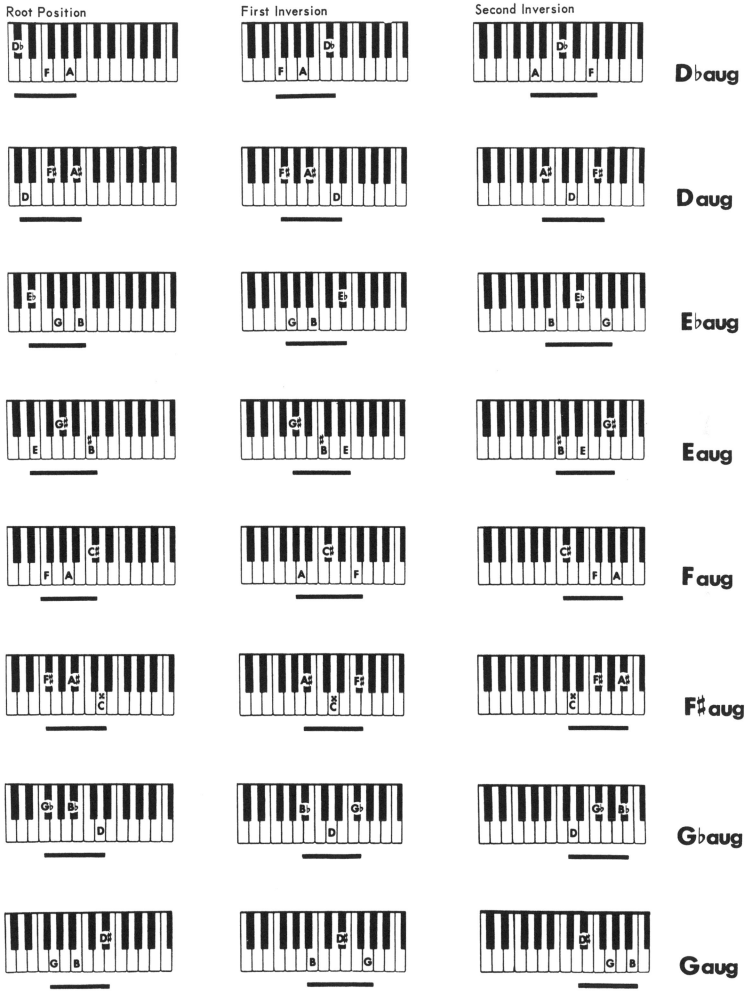

Root Position   First Inversion   Second Inversion

Dbaug

Daug

Ebaug

Eaug

Faug

F#aug

Gbaug

Gaug

KT 5-52R

AUGMENTED SEVENTH CHORDS
(C+7, C7+5, C7♯5, C7aug, C7aug5)

Root Position	First Inversion	Second Inversion	Third Inversion	
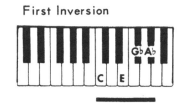	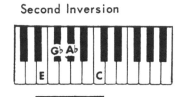	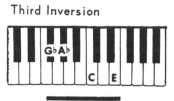		**A♭7♯5**
		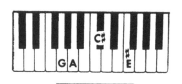		**A7♯5**
	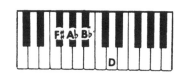	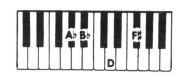		**B♭7♯5**
	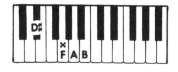	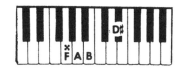	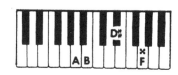	**B7♯5**
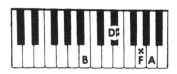		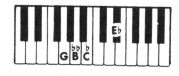		**C♭7♯5**
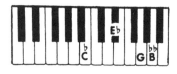				**C7♯5**
	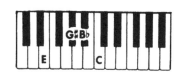		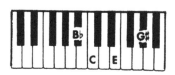	**C7♯5**
		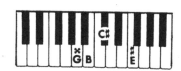	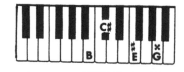	**C♯7♯5**

Consists of Root, Major Third, Augmented Fifth and Minor Seventh.

KT 5-52R

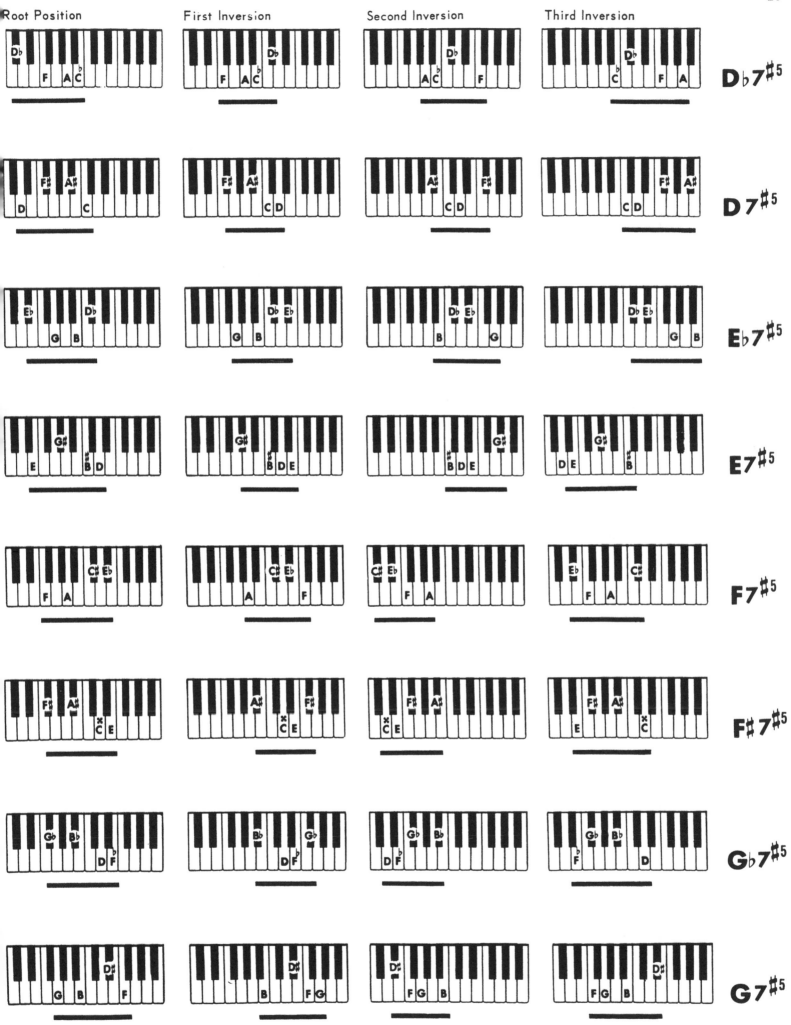

DIMINISHED CHORDS
(Cdim, C°)

Root Position   First Inversion   Second Inversion

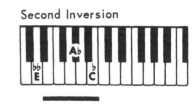

A♭dim

Adim

B♭dim

Bdim

C♭dim

Cdim

C♯dim

Consists of Root, Minor Third and Diminished Fifth.

KT 5-52R

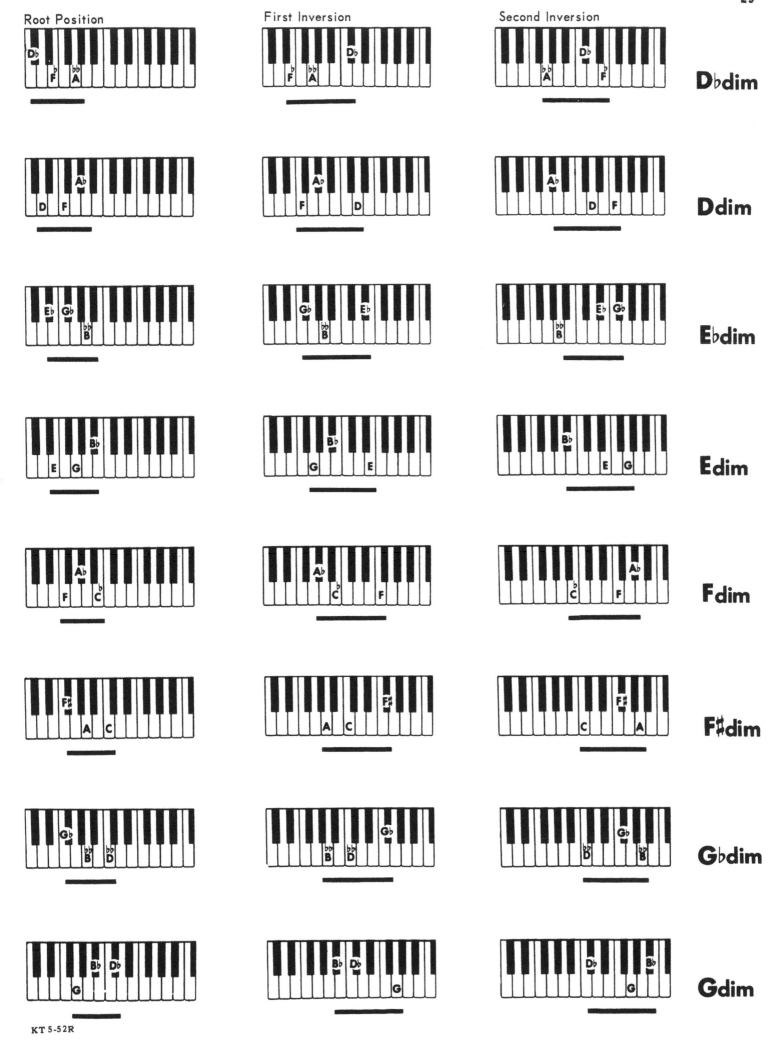

DIMINISHED SEVENTH CHORDS
(C dim7, C°7)

In reality, there are only three groups of Diminished Seventh Chords.
1. Abdim7, Bdim7, Cbdim7, Ddim7, Fdim7 and G#dim7.
2. Adim7, Cdim7, D#dim7, Ebdim7, F#dim7 and Gbdim7.
3. A#dim7, Bbdim7, C#dim7, Dbdim7, Edim7 and Gdim7.

Root Position   First Inversion   Second Inversion   Third Inversion

A♭°7

A°7

B♭°7

B°7

C♭°7

C°7

C#°7

*Rare. To keep the correct spelling of the Cbdim7 Chord, it is necessary to use a B triple flat. (Bbbb)
This chord consists of a Root, Minor Third, Diminished Fifth and Diminished Seventh.

KT 5-52R

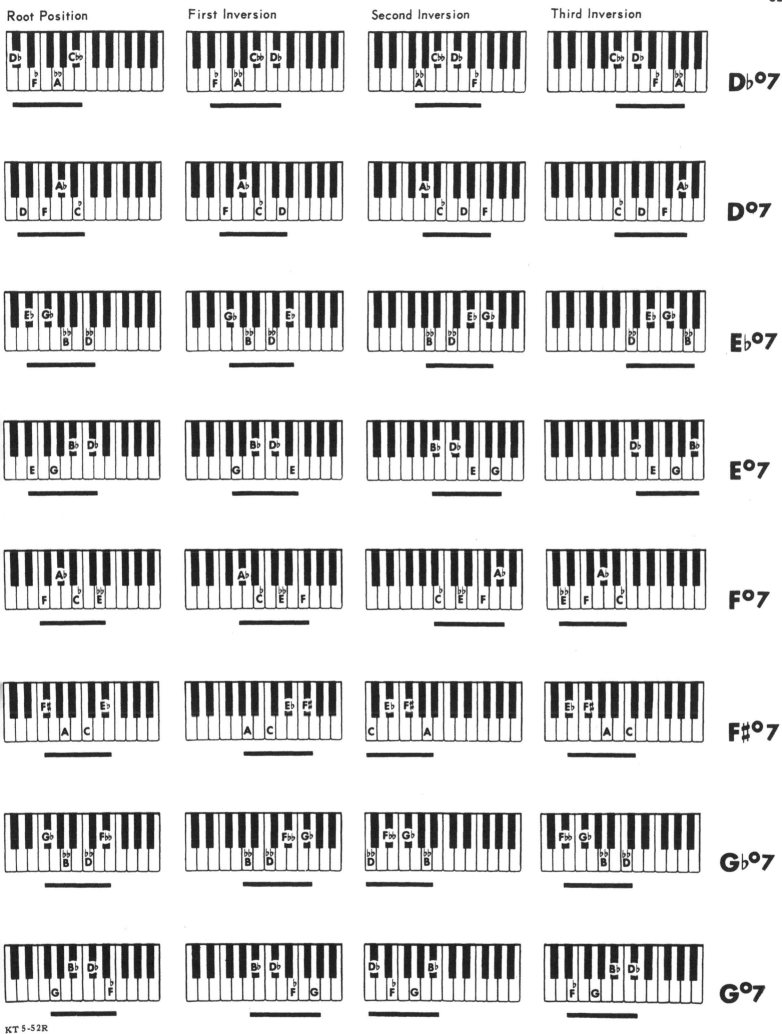

Root Position   First Inversion   Second Inversion   Third Inversion

Db°7

D°7

Eb°7

E°7

F°7

F#°7

Gb°7

G°7

KT 5-52R

MAJOR SEVENTH CHORDS
(CM7, Cma7, Cmaj7)

Root Position	First Inversion	Second Inversion	Third Inversion	
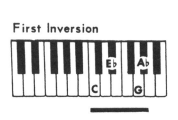		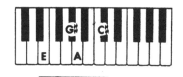	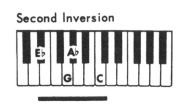	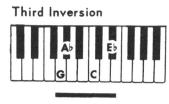 A♭M7
	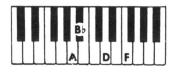		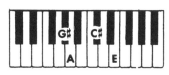	AM7
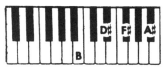				B♭M7
		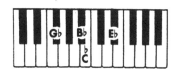		BM7
	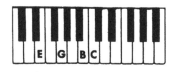			C♭M7
				CM7
				C♯M7

Consists of Root, Major Third, Perfect Fifth and Major Seventh.

KT 5-52R

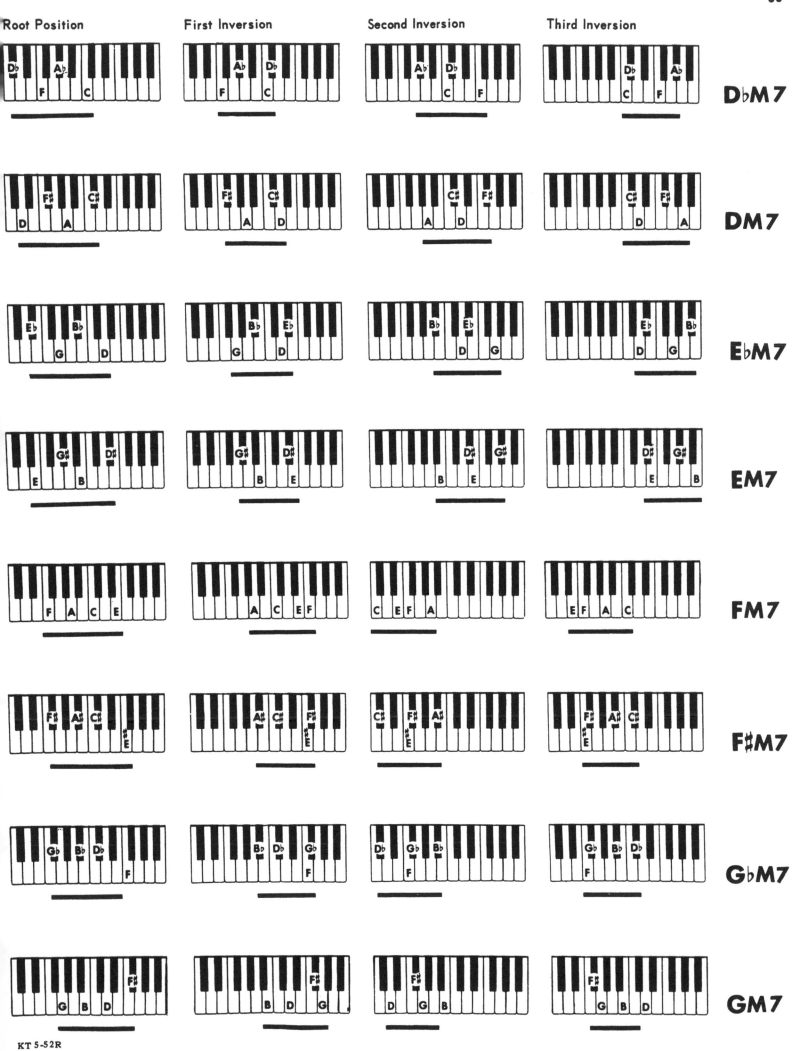

Root Position   First Inversion   Second Inversion   Third Inversion

D♭M7

DM7

E♭M7

EM7

FM7

F♯M7

G♭M7

GM7

KT 5-52R

MAJOR SEVENTH CHORDS WITH FLAT THIRD
(CM7b3, CM7-3, ma or maj used sometimes for M)

Root Position	First Inversion	Second Inversion	Third Inversion	
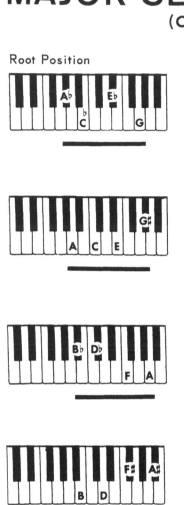				**AbM7b**
				AM7b
				BbM7b
				BM7b
				CbM7b
				CM7b3
				**C#M7**

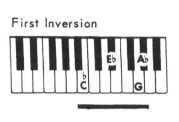 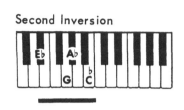  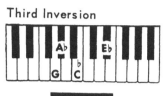
  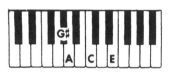

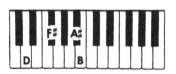  
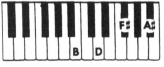 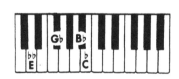  
 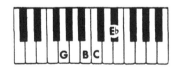 
 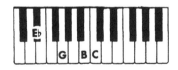  

Consists of Root, Minor Third, Perfect Fifth and Major Seventh.

KT 5-52R

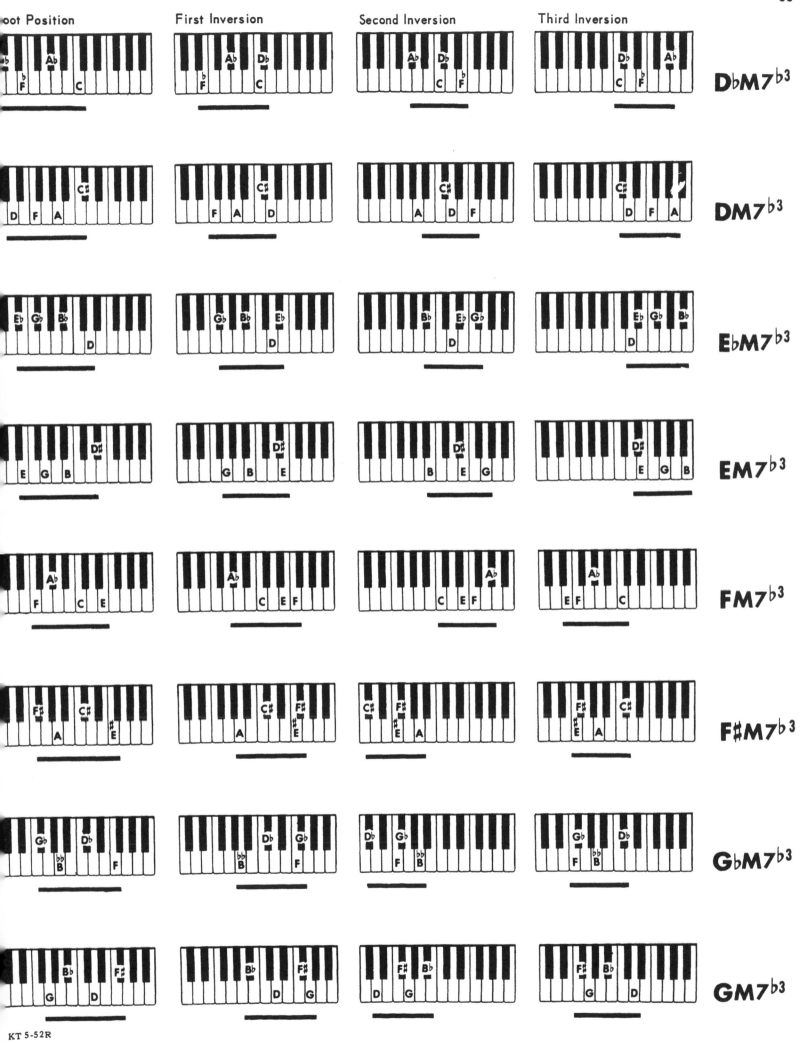

MAJOR SEVENTH CHORDS WITH FLAT FIFTH

(CM7b5, CM7-5, CM7-, ma or maj used sometimes for M)

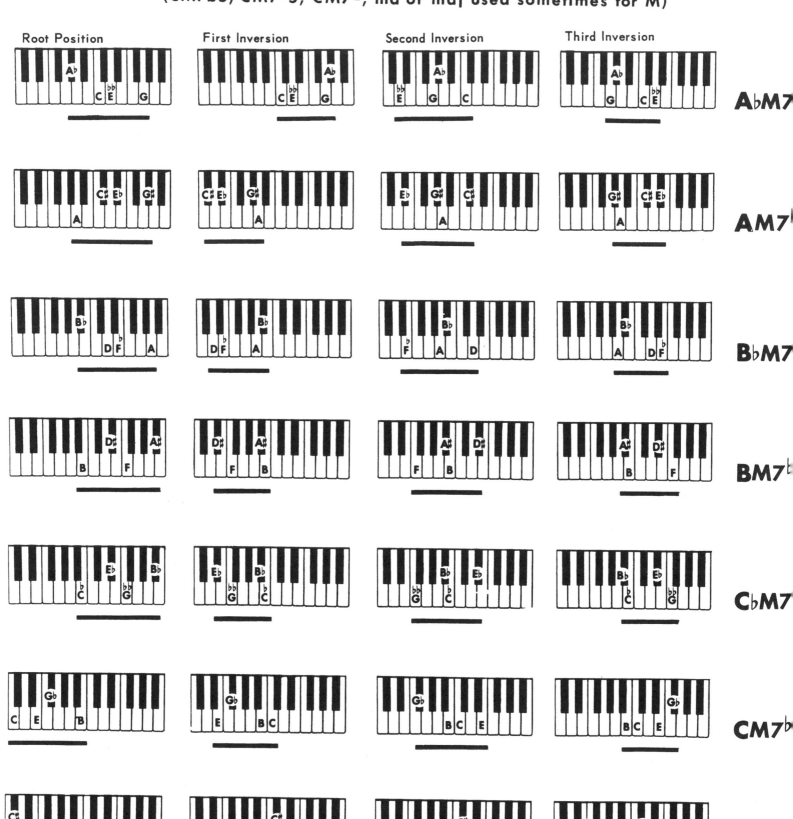

Consists of Root, Major Third, Diminished Fifth and Major Seventh.

KT 5-52R

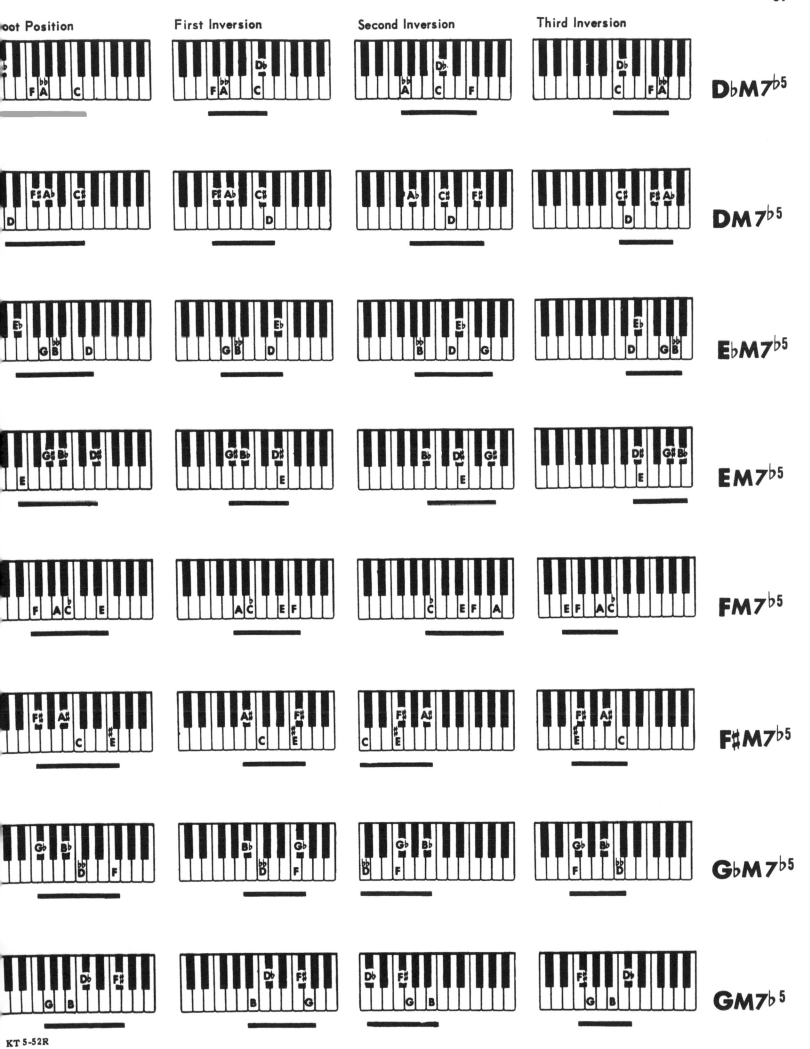

MAJOR SEVENTH CHORDS
WITH AUGMENTED FIFTH
(CM7+5, Cma 7+5, Cmaj7+5, ♯ used sometimes for +)

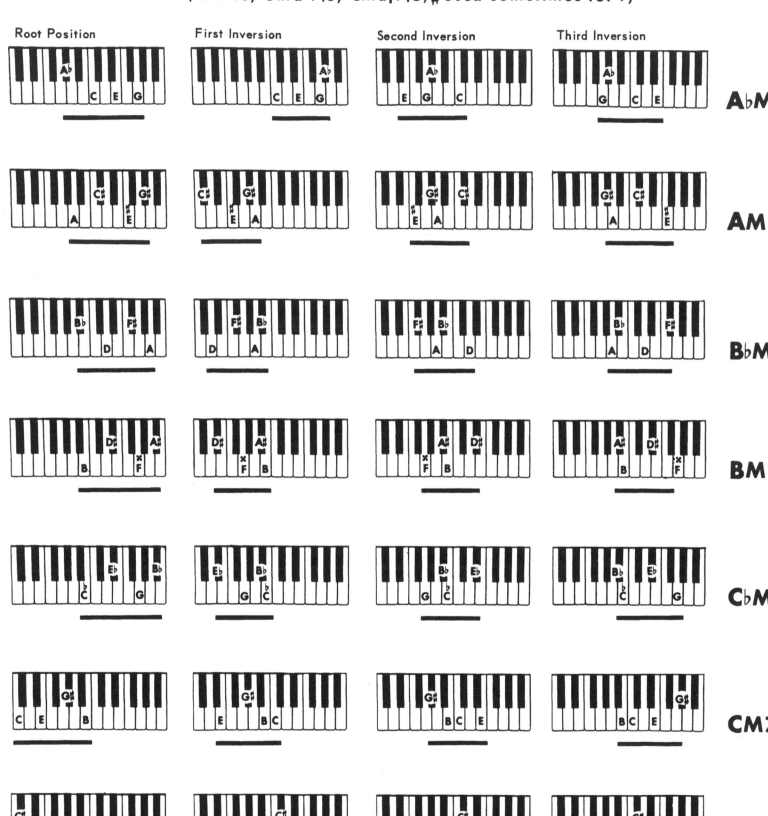

Consists of Root, Major Third, Augmented Fifth and Major Seventh.

KT 5-52R

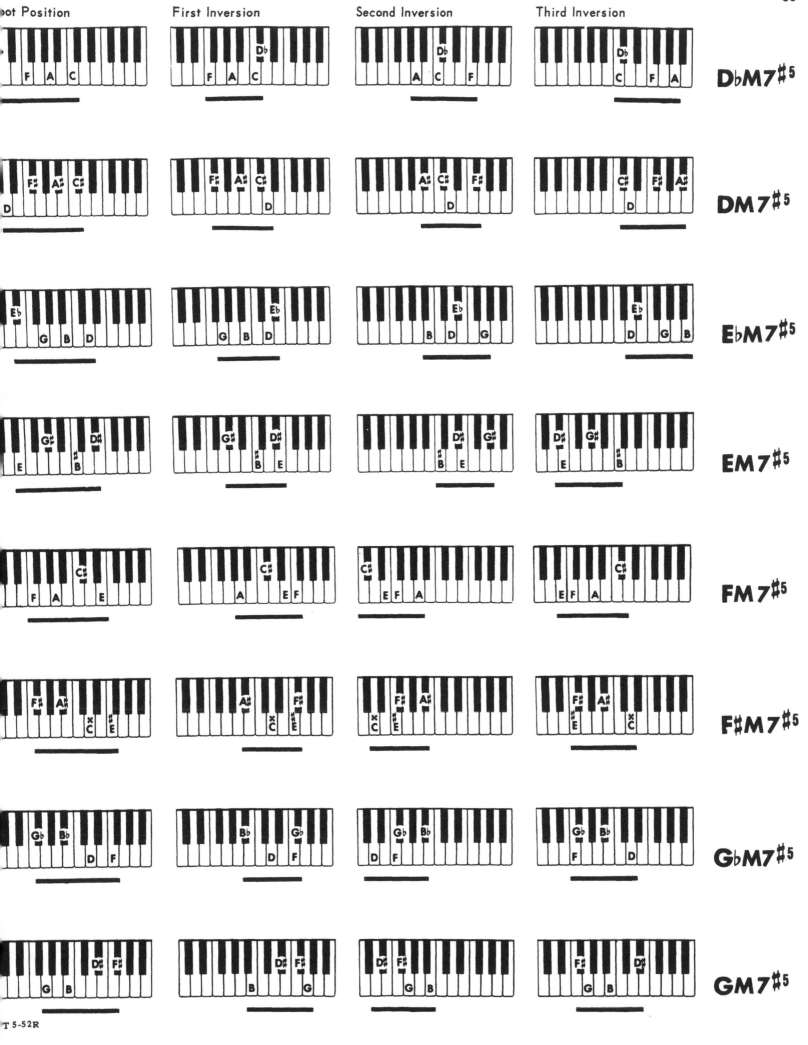

MAJOR SEVENTH CHORDS
WITH FLAT THIRD AND FLAT FIFTH

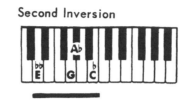
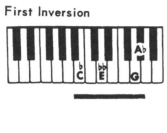

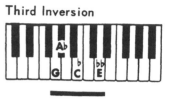

(CM7♭3/♭5, CM7−3/−5, ma or maj used sometimes for M)

Root Position	First Inversion	Second Inversion	Third Inversion	
				A♭M7♭♭
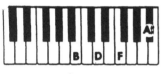				AM7♭3/♭5
				B♭M7♭♭
				BM7♭3/♭5
				C♭M7♭♭
				CM7♭3/♭5
				C♯M7♭♭

Consists of Root, Minor Third, Diminished Fifth and Major Seventh.

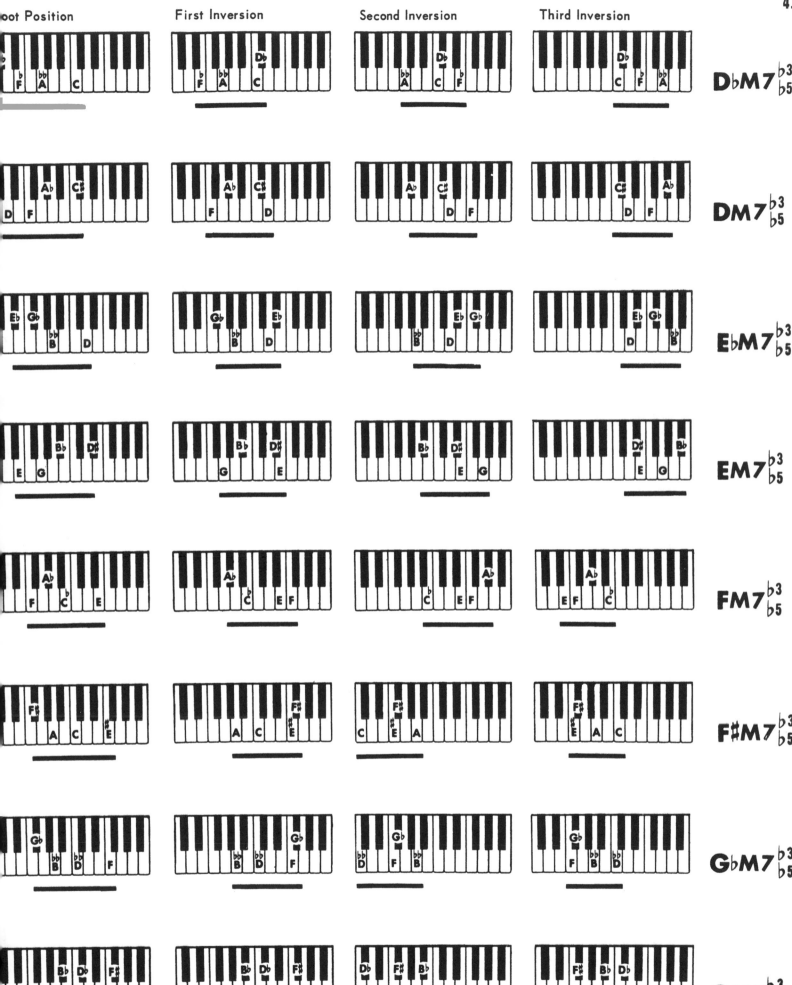

MAJOR SEVENTH CHORDS
WITH FLAT THIRD AND AUGMENTED FIFTH

(CM7$^{\flat 3}_{+5}$, CM7$^{-3}_{\sharp 5}$, ma or maj used sometimes for M)

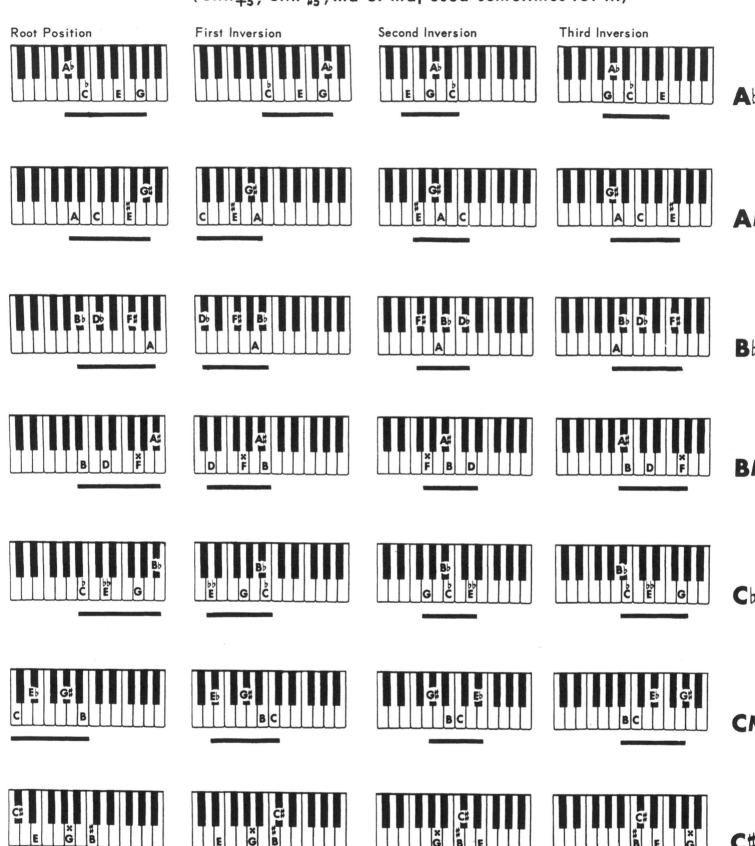

Consists of Root, Minor Third, Augmented Fifth and Major Seventh.

KT 5-52R

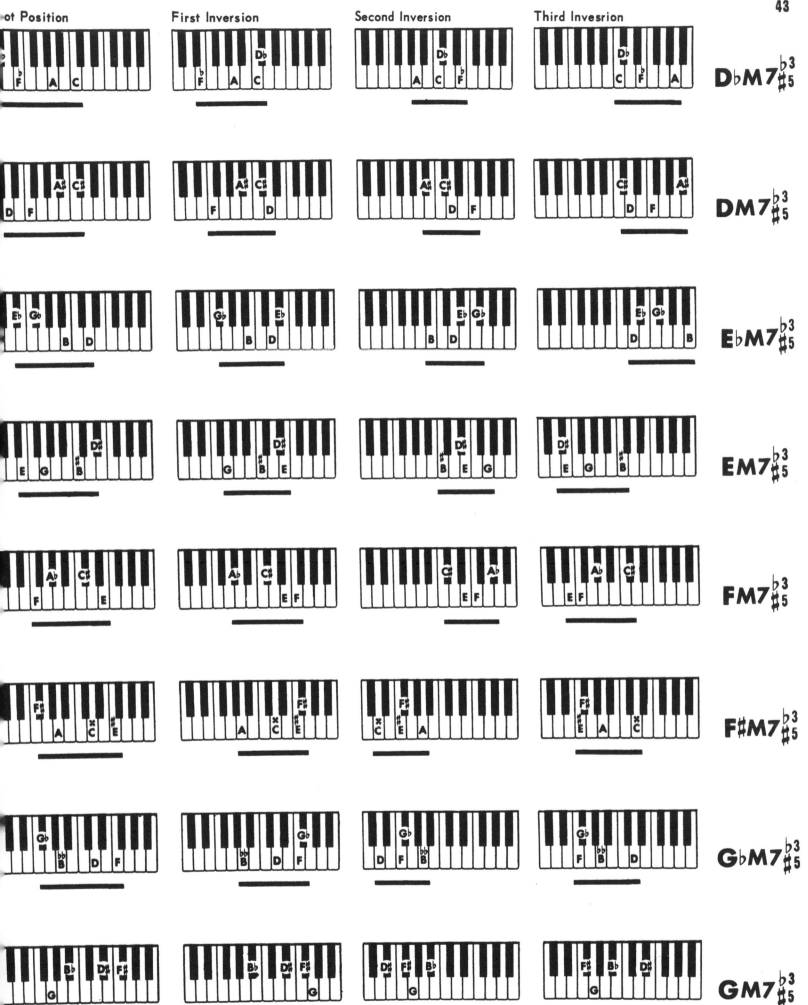

NINTH CHORDS

Ninth Chords are constructed by adding a third to the Seventh Chords, or the ninth scale degree which actually is the second scale degree.

Ninth Chord with Minor Seventh.

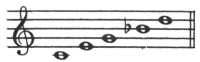

Ninth Chord with Major Seventh.

The Ninth can be lowered, thus made into a Minor Chord (b9,—9). The ninth can be raised, thus made into an Augmented Ninth Chord. (♯9,+9). The various alterations made with the Seventh Chords can also be made with the Ninth Chords. In doing so, if the Ninth is raised in a minor chord, it would be the same as the minor third. The chord, when played, is divided between the left and the right hand.

ELEVENTH CHORDS

Eleventh Chords are constructed by adding a third to the Ninth Chords, or the eleventh degree of the scale which in reality is the fourth degree of the scale.

Eleventh Chord with Minor Seventh.

Eleventh Chord with Major Seventh.

The Eleventh can be raised, thus made into an Augmented Eleventh Chord. (+11, ♯11). The eleventh tone is not lowered, if so it would double the third of the chord. The various alterations made with the Seventh and Ninth Chords can also be made with the Eleventh Chords as this is an extension of the two mentioned chords. This chord is divided between the left and the right hands. In using this chord the Third is usually omitted. In using the Augmented Eleventh Chord, the Fifth is sometimes omitted.

KT 5-52R

THIRTEENTH CHORDS

Thirteenth Chords are constructed by adding a Third to the Eleventh Chord, or the thirteenth scale degree which in reality is the sixth scale degree.

Thirteenth Chord with Minor Seventh.

Thirteenth Chord with Major Seventh.

This thirteenth scale degree can be raised and made into an Augmented Thirteenth Chord. (+13, ♯13). In doing so, if the Seventh of the chord is a minor seventh, it would only double this note. The Thirteenth can also be lowered, (b13, —13) but in doing so, if the Augmented Chord is used, it would only double the raised fifth note of the chord. The various alterations made with the Seventh, Ninth and Eleventh Chords can also be made with the Thirteenth Chords as this is an extension of these chords. This chord when played is divided between the two hands. Usually the Third and Fifth are omitted from this chord.

The Seventh, Ninth, Eleventh and Thirteenth Chords can be called "Superimposed Chords" due to having one chord over the other as well as mixed together.

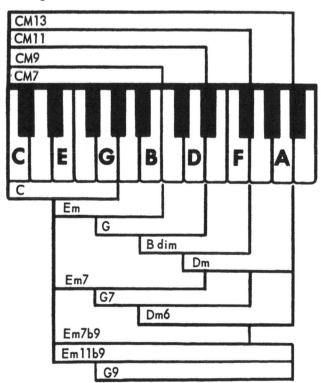

NINTH, ELEVENTH and THIRTEENTH CHORDS

As all these notes cannot be played with one hand, the notes of the chords are usually divided between both hands, pedal included, with organ. The various alterations applied with the previous chords may be used with these in many cases.

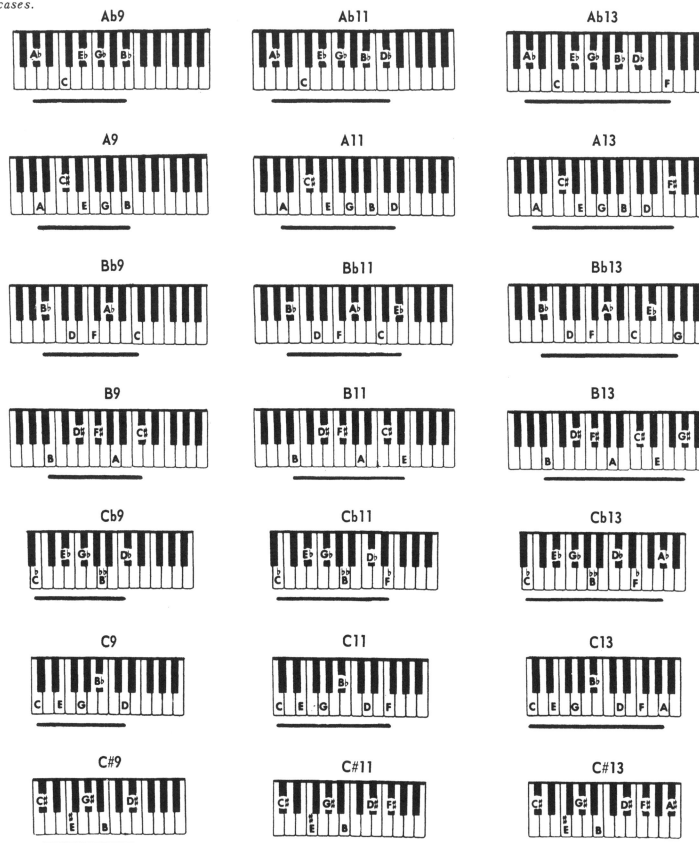

Consists of Root, Major Third, Perfect Fifth, Minor Seventh and Major Ninth.

Consists of Root, Major Third, Perfect Fifth, Minor Seventh, Major Ninth and Perfect Eleventh.

Consists of Root, Major Third, Perfect Fifth, Minor Seventh, Major Ninth, Perfect Eleventh and Major Thirteenth.

KT 5-52R

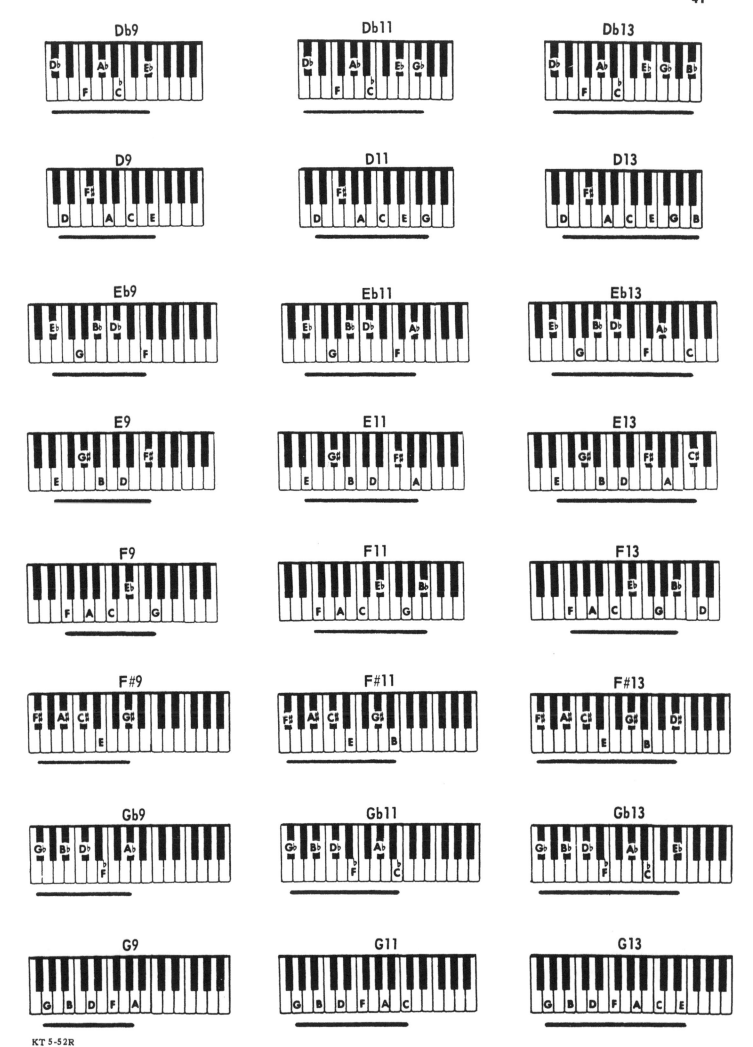

CHORD SYNONYMS

In a language, where one finds two words conveying the same meaning, so it is true of chords. Below one will find that each chord will have the same sound as the one next to it, even though the spelling of the chord may differ.

➔		←	➔		←	➔		←		
Abm7	=	B6	Ab7b5	=	D7b5	Abm6	=	Fm7b5	=	C#9
Abm7	=	Cb6	A7b5	=	Eb7b5	Abm6	=	Fm7b5	=	Db9
Am7	=	C6	Bb7b5	=	E7b5	Am6	=	F#m7b5	=	D9
Bbm7	=	C#6	B7b5	=	F7b5	Am6	=	Gbm7b5	=	D9
Bbm7	=	Db6	Cb7b5	=	F7b5	Bbm6	=	Gm7b5	=	Eb9
Bm7	=	D6	C7b5	=	F#7b5	Bm6	=	Abm7b5	=	E9
Cbm7	=	D6	C7b5	=	Gb7b5	Cbm6	=	Abm7b5	=	E9
Cm7	=	Eb6	C#7b5	=	G7b5	Cm6	=	Am7b5	=	F9
C#m7	=	E6	Db7b5	=	G7b5	C#m6	=	Bbm7b5	=	F#9
Dbm7	=	E6				Dbm6	=	Bbm7b5	=	Gb9
Dm7	=	F6				Dm6	=	Bm7b5	=	G9
Ebm7	=	Gb6				Ebm6	=	Cm7b5	=	Ab9
Ebm7	=	F#6				Em6	=	Dbm7b5	=	A9
Em7	=	G6				Em6	=	C#m7b5	=	A9
Fm7	=	Ab6				Fm6	=	Dm7b5	=	Bb9
F#m7	=	A6				F#m6	=	Ebm7b5	=	B9
Gbm7	=	A6				Gbm6	=	Ebm7b5	=	Cb9
Gm7	=	Bb6				Gm6	=	Em7b5	=	C9

b5 = −5 = °5 = dim5

For those with a limited knowledge of chords, the following will serve as a guide in chord usage. However, it is advisable to extend the use, in the knowledge of chords, to make ones' playing more interesting and professional sounding.

For a better understanding in the use of chords, the following books will help:— *CHORD PROGRESSIONS MADE EASY*,(either organ or piano) *THE CHORD APPROACH TO "POP" PIANO PLAYING* and *THE CHORD AP-PROACH TO "POP" ORGAN PLAYING*. Other chord books include *CHORD CHARTS, CHORD GUIDE, CHORD ENCYCLOPEDIA, POCKET DICTIONARY OF CHORDS* and *FAKE IT*. All of these are by Dr. Albert De Vito.

In the following, the C Chord is used as an example, but any other chord may serve as a substitution.
C7, C9, C6, Cmaj7, C7−9, Cmaj7/9, C11, C13:— A C Chord may be used.
Cm7, Cm6, Cmaj7−3, C9−3, C11−3, C13−3:— A C Minor Chord may be used. (−3 is used for a minor 3rd.)
C9, C11, C13:— A C7 Chord may be used.
C7aug5, C9aug5, Caug11:— A C7 Chord may be used without the 5th or an C aug.
C7−5:— A C7 Chord may be used without the 5th.

With experimentation, one could find other examples. Much will depend upon the melody. For a good basic background, it is suggested that one learns all the Major, Minor, Augmented and Diminished Chords. This will not be as difficult as it may seem as there are only four Augmented Chords and only three Diminished Seventh Chords.

MAJOR SCALES

As music is written using *Semitones* and *Whole Tones*, it is advisable to understand them. A *Semitone* is sometime refered to as a *Half Step* and a *Whole Tone* is sometime refered to as a *Whole Step*. A *Semitone* or *Half Step* is the very next key (on keyboard instruments) either to the right or left. It may be either a black or a white key.

A *Whole Tone*, or a *Whole Step* consists of two *Semitones*. It may be either to the right or left of a given key. A point to remember:– There is always one key between, either black or white. Please see following diagrams.

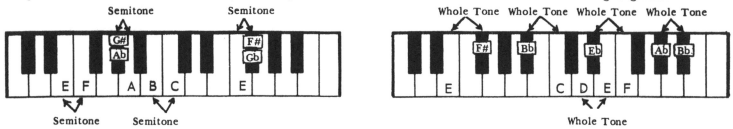

The following scale, C major scale (actually it could be any one of the fifteen major scales listed below) show the various degrees of the scale (1, 3, 5, 7, 9, 11 and 13) from which the many chords are constructed. Notice every other note in the scale is used with the exception of the ''6th''. Also notice in going to the ''13th'' that every note in the scale is included.

All Major Scales are constructed in the following manner:– Whole Step, Whole Step, Half Step, Whole Step, Whole Step, Whole Step and Half Step. Please see C Major Scale below for a better understanding.

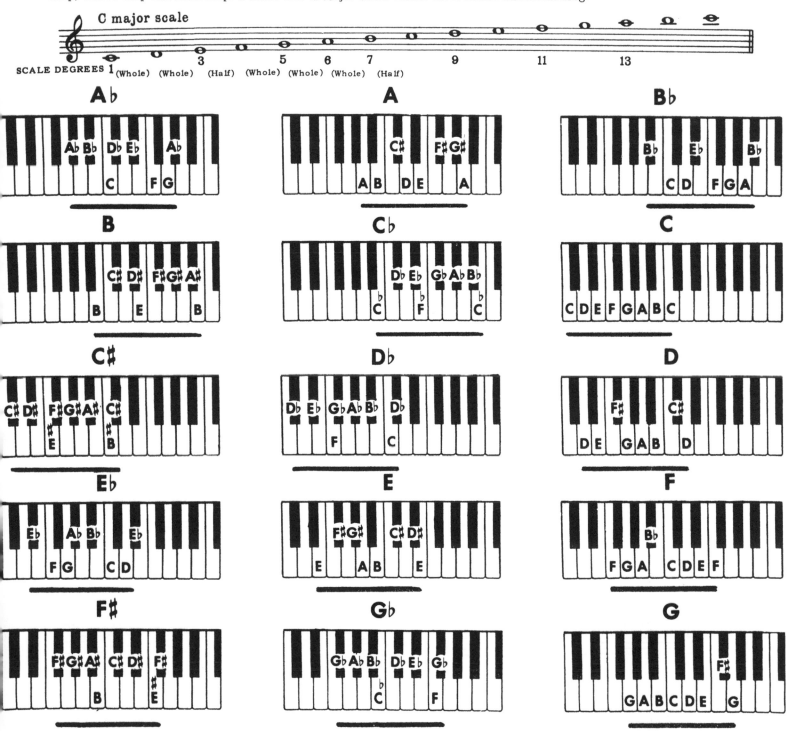

MAJOR SCALES

In the following Major Scales, the formation is shown for forming chords based upon the scale degrees. The 1st, 3rd and 5th degree of each major scale form a Major Chord, named after the note of the 1st degree. If the first degree is C, it will be a C major chord. If the first degree is F, it will be a F major chord. The 1st, 3rd, 5th and 7th degrees will form a Major Seventh Chord. The 1st, 3rd, 5th, 7th and 9th degrees will form a Ninth Chord with a major seventh. The Eleventh Chord, with a major seventh is formed by the 1st, 3rd, 5th, 7th, 9th and 11th. The Thirteenth Chord, with a major seventh is formed by the 1st, 3rd, 5th, 7th, 9th, 11th and the 13th.

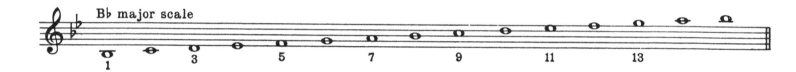

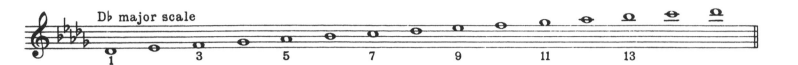

Db major scale

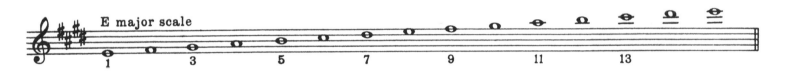

D major scale

Eb major scale

E major scale

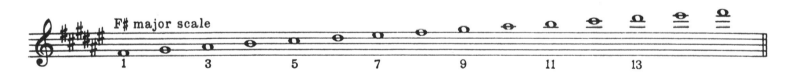

F major scale

F# major scale

Gb major scale

G major scale

EUROPEAN CHORD SYMBOLS

Rather than using Chord Symbols as C, Cm, C7 as the U.S.A., some European Countries use Scale Degrees instead. The + indicates a Major Chord and the − indicates a Minor Chord. Please see the following examples.

DOb +	= Cb	DOb −	= Cb m	DOb +7	= Cb 7	DOb −7	= Cb m7
DO +	= C	DO −	= Cm	DO +7	= C7	DO −7	= Cm7
DO♯ +	= C♯	DO♯ −	= C♯m	DO♯ +7	= C♯7	DO♯ −7	= C♯m7
REb +	= Db	REb −	= Db m	REb +7	= Db7	REb −7	= Db m7
RE +	= D	RE −	= Dm	RE +7	= D7	RE −7	= Dm7
MIb +	= Eb	MIb −	= Eb m	MIb +7	= Eb 7	MIb −7	= Ebm7
MI +	= E	MI−	= Em	MI +7	= E7	MI −7	= Em7
FA+	= F	FA −	= Fm	FA +7	= F7	FA −7	= Fm7
FA♯ +	= F♯	FA♯ −	= F♯m	FA♯ +7	= F♯7	FA♯ −7	= F♯m7
SOLb +	= Gb	SOLb −	= Gb m	SOLb +7	= Gb7	SOLb −7	= Gb m7
SOL +	= G	SOL −	= Gm	SOL +7	= G7	SOL −7	= Gm7
LAb+	= Ab	LAb −	= Ab m	LAb +7	= Ab 7	LAb −7	= Ab m7
LA +	= A	LA −	= Am	LAb +7	= A7	LA −7	= Am7
SIb +	= Bb	SIb −	= Bb m	SIb +7	= Bb 7	SIb −7	= Bb m7
SI +	= B	SI −	= Bm	SI +7	= B7	SI −7	= Bm7

CYCLE OF KEYS

MAJOR and MINOR KEY SIGNATURES

* (Bracketed Key Signatures sound alike and are called Enharmonic Keys.)